DUCK, HERE COMES ANOTHER DAY!

To KYLE
From WAYNE
Til 2000

DUCK, HERE COMES ANOTHER DAY!

by Charles M. Schulz

An Owl Book
Henry Holt and Company/ New York

Henry Holt and Company, Inc.
Publishers since 1866
115 West 18th Street
New York, New York 10011

Henry Holt® is a registered trademark
of Henry Holt and Company, Inc.

Published in Canada by Fitzhenry & Whiteside Ltd.,
195 Allstate Parkway, Markham, Ontario L3R 4T8.

Library of Congress Catalog Card Number: 94-73311

ISBN 0-8050-3570-2 (An Owl Book: pbk.)

Henry Holt books are available for special promotions
and premiums. For details contact: Director, Special Markets

Originally published by Holt, Rinehart and Winston in two
expanded editions under the titles *Don't Hassle Me
With Your Sighs, Chuck* in 1976 and *Speak Softly and
Carry a Beagle* in 1975.

New Owl Book Edition—1994

Printed in the United States of America
All first editions are printed on acid-free paper.∞

3 5 7 9 10 8 6 4 2

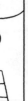

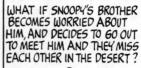

GO OUT IN THE KITCHEN, AND GET ME A DISH OF ICE CREAM

SAY, "PLEASE"

I'D KILL MYSELF BEFORE I'D SAY, "PLEASE"!!

HERE YOU ARE...

YOU DIDN'T SAY, "THANK YOU"

I'D RATHER DIE !!!

I'M KIND OF TIRED..I THINK I'LL GO TO BED

YOU DIDN'T SAY, "PLEASANT DREAMS"

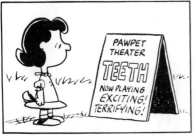

WHAT IF I KICK IT OVER YOUR HEAD, SIR?

WHAT IF SOME MAJOR LEAGUE SCOUT SPOTS ME, AND HIRES ME FOR HIS TEAM, AND I HAVE TO GO TO THE SUPER BOWL? WHAT WOULD I DO ABOUT SCHOOL?

JUST SHUT UP, MARCIE, AND KICK THE BALL!

DON'T BE IMPATIENT WITH ME, SIR...

OKAY, BALL, BEFORE I KICK YOU, I WANT TO APOLOGIZE...

I WANT YOU TO KNOW THERE'S NOTHING PERSONAL IN THIS, THAT I INTEND YOU NO HARM, THAT I HOPE THIS KICK DOES YOU NO INJURY, AND THAT...

KICK THE BALL, MARCIE!!

PATIENCE, SIR! THESE ARE THINGS WHICH MUST BE SAID!

HERE'S SOMETHING TO THINK ABOUT...

PICTURE THIS, IF YOU WILL...

YOU AND I ARE A NEWLY MARRIED COUPLE, SEE, AND YOU HAVE BEEN INVITED TO MOSCOW TO PARTICIPATE IN A PIANO COMPETITION...

YOU PERFORM BRILLIANTLY, BUT YOU LOSE! WHEN YOU ARE ASKED TO SAY A FEW WORDS TO THE PRESS, YOU ARE EXTREMELY GRACIOUS...

" I DON'T MIND LOSING," YOU SAY, "BECAUSE, AFTER ALL, I HAVE JUST MARRIED THE MOST WONDERFUL GIRL IN THE WORLD, AND SHE WILL ALWAYS BE MY PRIZE!"

HAHAHAHAHAHAHAHA

✳ SIGH ✳

IN THE ENTIRE HISTORY OF THE WORLD, THERE'S NO RECORD OF SANTA CLAUS EVER FILLING THE STOCKING OF A BIRD...

BUT THAT DOESN'T DISCOURAGE WOODSTOCK..

HE FEELS THE ODDS ARE WITH HIM!

THE ORANGE WAS A GOOD IDEA, WASN'T IT?

I FIGURE IF YOU PUT THE ORANGE IN WOODSTOCK'S CHRISTMAS STOCKING, IT WILL MAKE HIM VERY HAPPY

I'M GLAD YOU AGREE THAT THE ORANGE IS A GOOD IDEA

THE ORANGE WAS A GREAT IDEA...EXCEPT I ATE IT!

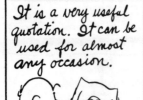

THAT'S FRENCH TOAST...GO AHEAD, AND TRY IT... THERE'S NOTHING TO BE AFRAID OF

THERE MIGHT BE ONE SLIGHT PROBLEM

THE SYRUP MAY STICK TO YOUR FEET...

"SCHOOL BUILDING COLLAPSES DURING NIGHT!" GOOD GRIEF!

DON'T BOTHER TO GET UP, SALLY...OUR SCHOOL FELL OVER LAST NIGHT! LISTEN TO THIS...

I HAD ALL I COULD TAKE!

SCHOOL! SCHOOL! SCHOOL! SCHOOL!

WHY DID YOU DO IT ?!! WHY DID YOU DO IT ?!!

OUR POOR SCHOOL...WHY DO THINGS LIKE THIS HAVE TO HAPPEN? SUCH A BEAUTIFUL SCHOOL...NOW, JUST A PILE OF RUBBLE!

LOVE ME, LOVE MY RUBBLE!

HEY!

ARE YOU THE CRAZY LITTLE KID I'VE HEARD ABOUT WHO TALKS TO SCHOOL BUILDINGS?

GET AWAY FROM ME, MUSCLE HEAD OR I'LL PUNCH YOUR LIGHTS OUT!!

ANYWAY, HE WAS A GOOD SCHOOL, AND HE ALWAYS SPOKE VERY HIGHLY OF YOU

THAT'S NICE TO KNOW

IF YOU KNOW AN ANSWER AND I DON'T, YOU TELL ME WHAT IT IS, CHUCK

IF I KNOW AN ANSWER AND YOU DON'T, I'LL TELL YOU WHAT IT IS, OKAY?

WHAT HAPPENS IF NEITHER OF US KNOWS THE ANSWER?

WE'LL PUNT!

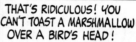

I HEAR YOUR FRIEND HAS A VAPOR LOCK

NOT A VAPOR LOCK! HE HAS "THE VAPORS"!!

NOW I KNOW WHY HOSPITAL VISITING HOURS ARE SO SHORT!

I HEAR YOUR FRIEND HAS THE VAPORS

YOU'RE TAKING AN AWFUL CHANCE TREATING HIM YOURSELF! WHAT IF SOMETHING GOES WRONG? HE COULD SUE YOU!

SUE ME?! WOODSTOCK WOULD NEVER DO THAT!

I WISH THEY'D HURRY UP, AND REBUILD OUR SCHOOL...

IF I HAVE TO SHARE A DESK WITH PEPPERMINT PATTY MUCH LONGER, I'LL BE BACK IN KINDERGARTEN!

WHY DON'T YOU JUST TELL HER YOU DON'T WANT TO SIT WITH HER ANY MORE?

IF SHE GETS MAD, AND HITS YOU HARD ENOUGH, YOU WON'T HAVE TO GO TO SCHOOL AT ALL!

THE ANSWER IS SIX!

THREE!

YOU CONTRADICTED ME, CHUCK! YOU MADE A FOOL OUT OF ME IN FRONT OF THE WHOLE CLASS!

"SIX" WAS THE WRONG ANSWER... I **HAD** TO SAY, "THREE"

YOU DON'T LIKE ME, DO YOU, CHUCK?

DON'T BREATHE THROUGH YOUR MOUTH, CHUCK!

DON'T LICK YOUR FINGERS WHEN YOU TURN THE PAGES, CHUCK, AND DON'T SCRAPE YOUR FEET ON THE DESK...

WILL YOU STOP CRITICIZING ME?!

ANOTHER FINE MESS YOU'VE GOTTEN ME INTO, CHUCK!

PRINCIPAL'S OFFICE

YES, SIR, MR. PRINCIPAL

YOU WANT US TO WRITE ONE HUNDRED TIMES, "I WILL NOT CREATE A DISTURBANCE IN CLASS"?

ARE YOU AWARE, SIR, THAT MANY EDUCATORS FEEL THIS TO BE A VERY WRONG WAY TO PUNISH STUDENTS?

OH, NO, SIR... I'M NOT COMPLAINING... IT'S A WHOLE LOT BETTER THAN A RAP ON THE HEAD!

SUPPER-TIME!!

AAUGH!

WHAT HAPPENED? DID HE HURT HIS FOOT?

HE WAS GREEDY... HE TRIPPED OVER HIS OWN SUPPER DISH...

I'M DYING!

IT HAPPENS ALL THE TIME... THE SINS OF THE STOMACH ARE VISITED UNTO THE FOOT!

OH, SHUT UP!

GOOD GRIEF! WHAT HAPPENED TO YOU?

WELL, THERE WERE THESE THREE AIRLINE STEWARDESSES, SEE, AND THEY WERE ON RUNAWAY HORSES, SEE, AND I HAD TO SAVE THEM...

I HEARD YOU TRIPPED OVER YOUR SUPPER DISH...

AS SOON AS I GET MY CRUTCHES, I'M GOING TO START HITTING PEOPLE!

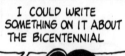

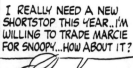

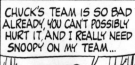

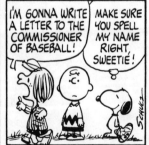

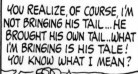

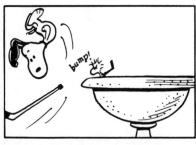

I DIDN'T KNOW YOU COULD SKATE, SIR!

I'M REALLY INTO SPORTS, MARCIE.. IT'S MY LIFE...WHEN I GROW UP, I'M GONNA PLAY PROFESSIONAL BALL IN THE SUMMER AND SKATE, IN AN ICE SHOW IN THE WINTER...

DURING THE OFF-SEASON, I'LL PROBABLY DO A LITTLE BOWLING OR POP A WHEELIE IN A MOTO-CROSS...

YOU'RE AN AMAZING PERSON, SIR

STOP CALLING ME "SIR"!

YOU KNOW WHAT I MISS, MARCIE? I MISS NOT HAVING A "SKATING MOTHER"

SKATING MOTHERS ARE LIKE STAGE MOTHERS AND SWIMMING MOTHERS...

THEY GRUMBLE AND COMPLAIN AND GOSSIP AND FUSS, BUT YOU SURE NEED THEM!

HOW DO THEY GET THAT WAY, SIR?

EARLY RISING AND TOO MUCH COFFEE!

MARCIE! YOU HAVE A SEWING MACHINE!

IT'S NOT MINE, SIR.. IT'S MY MOTHER'S

WHY DON'T YOU MAKE ME A SKATING OUTFIT, MARCIE?

I DON'T KNOW HOW TO SEW, SIR...

I WANT TO LOOK BEAUTIFUL FOR THE SKATING COMPETITION.. HOW ABOUT A RED SKATING DRESS?

THAT'S IT! YOU CAN MAKE ME A RED OUTFIT WITH LOTS OF SEQUINS!

YOU'RE NOT MUCH FOR LISTENING ARE YOU, SIR?

YES, MA'AM... WE WANT TO BUY SOME MATERIAL FOR A SKATING DRESS...

MY LITTLE FRIEND HERE HAS VOLUNTEERED TO MAKE ME A SKATING OUTFIT FOR A COMPETITION I'M GOING TO BE IN!

OH, AND BEFORE I FORGET IT, WE'LL NEED ABOUT A MILLION SEQUINS! WHEN I'M OUT THERE DOING MY NUMBER, I WANT TO REALLY SPARKLE!

AREN'T YOU EXCITED, MARCIE?!

MY STOMACH HURTS CLEAR DOWN TO MY TOES!

POLYESTER DOUBLE-KNIT? THAT'S TOO EXPENSIVE MA'AM

HOW ABOUT DENIM? I'LL BET MY LITTLE FRIEND HERE COULD MAKE ME A NEAT SKATING DRESS OUT OF DENIM! SHE'S A GREAT SEWER!

DON'T WORRY ABOUT STRETCHING.. WE'LL JUST THROW IN A FEW GUSSETS!

HOW'RE YOUR GUSSETS, MARCIE?

GUSSETS?

OKAY, SIR, I THINK I HAVE ALL YOUR MEASUREMENTS

THE WAY I SEE IT, YOU'RE A SIZE EIGHT... YOUR WAIST IS TWENTY-THREE INCHES, YOUR HIPS ARE TWENTY-EIGHT INCHES...

AND YOUR.....YOUR.....UH... YOUR.........YOUR......

"BUST," MARCIE!! IT'S A PERFECTLY LEGITIMATE SEWING TERM!

TWENTY-SIX INCHES, SIR!

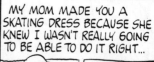

IF I'M GONNA LOOK NICE FOR THE SKATING COMPETITION, MARCIE, YOU'LL HAVE TO HELP ME WITH MY HAIR...

WELL, PERHAPS WE COULD SORT OF PULL IT BACK A LITTLE ON BOTH SIDES, SIR, AND FASTEN IT WITH RUBBER BANDS...

IF IT DOESN'T WORK OUT, WE CAN ALWAYS TRY SOMETHING ELSE...

SOMETHING ELSE?

SOMETHING ELSE!!

IT'S NO USE, SIR...I CAN'T FIX YOUR HAIR!

MAYBE I SHOULD GO OVER TO SEE CHUCK'S DAD...HE'S A BARBER, AND SEEING AS HOW I'M CHUCK'S FRIEND, MAYBE HE'LL GIVE ME A DISCOUNT...

IF I HAD BEEN BORN BEAUTIFUL, I WOULDN'T HAVE TO GO THROUGH ALL THIS...

ALL MY LIFE I'VE DREAMED OF LOOKING LIKE PEGGY FLEMING...INSTEAD, I LOOK LIKE BABE RUTH!

Once there were two mice who lived in a museum.

One evening after the museum had closed, the first mouse crawled into a huge suit of armor.

Before he knew it, he was lost. "Help!" he shouted to his friend.

"Help me make it through the knight!"

I JUST REMEMBERED SOMETHING, SNOOPY...

I STILL OWE YOU FOR MY SKATING LESSONS, DON'T I?

WELL, I DON'T HAVE ANY MONEY, BUT I HAVE SOMETHING ELSE THAT I CAN GIVE YOU...

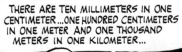

DUCK, BIG BROTHER! HERE COMES ANOTHER DAY!!

I MUST HAVE A GOOD IMAGINATION...

I THOUGHT I HEARD YOU GIGGLING THIS MORNING...

IT'S THAT STUPID CUSTODIAN WITH HIS MOP...

IT TICKLES!

TOMORROW IS BEETHOVEN'S BIRTHDAY... WHAT ARE YOU GOING TO BUY ME?

I'M NOT GOING TO BUY YOU ANYTHING!

YOU KNOW WHY? BECAUSE YOU DON'T CARE ANYTHING ABOUT BEETHOVEN! YOU NEVER HAVE!!

YOU DON'T CARE THAT HE SUFFERED! YOU DON'T CARE THAT HIS STOMACH HURT AND THAT HE COULDN'T HEAR!

YOU NEVER CARED THAT THE COUNTESS TURNED HIM DOWN, OR THAT THERESE MARRIED THE BARON INSTEAD OF HIM OR THAT LOBKOWITZ STOPPED HIS ANNUITY!!

IF THE COUNTESS HADN'T TURNED HIM DOWN, WOULD YOU BUY ME SOMETHING?

The Gift

It was the holiday season.

She and her husband had decided to attend a performance of King Lear.

It was their first night out together in months.

During the second act one of the performers became ill.

The manager of the theater walked onto the stage, and asked, "Is there a doctor in the house?"

Her husband stood up, and shouted, "I have an honorary degree from Anderson College!"

It was at that moment when she decided not to get him anything for Christmas.

SCHULZ

STUPID DOG!

NEW YEAR'S WAS FIVE DAYS AGO, AND THAT DOG IS STILL CELEBRATING!

TALK ABOUT BEING LATE...LET ME SHOW YOU SOMETHING...

MY DUMB BROTHER HERE IS JUST GETTING AROUND TO ADDRESSING HIS CHRISTMAS CARDS!

NOBODY COULD BE LATER THAN THAT!

KNOCK KNOCK KNOCK

TRICK OR TREAT?!

HOW ABOUT A SKATE, SWEETIE?

HOW ABOUT A SKATE, SWEETIE?

CHEAP SHOT!

RATS!

IT'S TWO O'CLOCK IN THE MORNING, AND I'M WIDE AWAKE...

WHERE AM I GOING? WHAT AM I DOING? WHAT IS THE MEANING OF LIFE?

BAM BAM BAM BAM

I RECOGNIZE THAT KICK...THAT'S THE KICK OF SOMEONE WHO HAS AWAKENED IN THE MIDDLE OF THE NIGHT, AND WANTS TO KNOW THE MEANING OF LIFE...

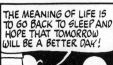

THE MEANING OF LIFE IS TO GO BACK TO SLEEP AND HOPE THAT TOMORROW WILL BE A BETTER DAY!

AND IF YOU'RE THINKING ABOUT EATING, FORGET IT!!

SLAM!!

WOULDN'T THAT UNPLUG YOUR HEATING PAD!!

SCHULZ

YES, MA'AM, I'M READY...

FOR MY NATURE REPORT TODAY, I AM BRINGING YOU AN EXCLUSIVE!

ROCK SNAKES!!

WHAT, YOU MAY ASK, IS A ROCK SNAKE? THAT IS A GOOD QUESTION! A ROCK SNAKE IS A SNAKE THAT SNEAKS UP BEHIND YOU, AND THROWS A ROCK AT YOU!

NOW, HERE IS MY EXCLUSIVE...IT USED TO BE THOUGHT THAT ROCK SNAKES WERE DANGEROUS, BUT MY AUTHORITY SAYS THIS IS NOT SO...

A ROCK SNAKE CANNOT THROW VERY HIGH, YOU SEE, SO THEREFORE, ALL HE CAN DO IS HIT YOU ON THE BACK OF THE LEG...SO SAYS MY AUTHORITY!

MA'AM?

LINUS VAN PELT.... YES, MA'AM..

SHE SAID SHE REMEMBERS YOU FROM WHEN YOU WERE IN HER CLASS!

I HAVE A PROBLEM, CHUCK... I KEEP FALLING ASLEEP IN SCHOOL...

MY DAD HAS THIS NIGHT JOB, SEE, AND HE DOESN'T GET HOME UNTIL TWO IN THE MORNING...

I'M AFRAID TO GO TO SLEEP WHILE I'M ALONE IN THE HOUSE SO I'VE BEEN SITTING UP WATCHING TV...

YOU NEED SOMEONE TO STAY WITH YOU...

HOW ABOUT A WATCH-BEAGLE?

I APPRECIATE YOUR COMING TO STAY WITH ME, SNOOPY..

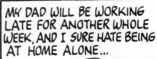

MY DAD WILL BE WORKING LATE FOR ANOTHER WHOLE WEEK, AND I SURE HATE BEING AT HOME ALONE...

I'VE BEEN FALLING ASLEEP IN SCHOOL BECAUSE I'M AFRAID TO GO TO BED AT NIGHT! NOW, I'LL FEEL SAFE BECAUSE I'LL KNOW YOU'RE GUARDING ME, AND...

Z

I REALLY APPRECIATE YOUR COMING OVER TO STAY WITH ME, SNOOPY...

MY DAD WILL BE WORKING LATE FOR ANOTHER WEEK, AND I SURE GET SCARED BEING IN THE HOUSE ALONE..

C'MON, I'LL SHOW YOU OUR GUEST ROOM...YOU'LL HAVE IT ALL TO YOURSELF...

AND I HOPE YOU'LL LIKE THE WATERBED...

I SURE FEEL SAFER WITH SNOOPY IN THE HOUSE..

MAYBE I CAN GET A GOOD NIGHT'S SLEEP FOR ONCE, AND NOT FEEL SO TIRED IN SCHOOL TOMORROW..

ONCE OL' SNOOP GETS USED TO THE WATERBED IN THE GUEST ROOM, I KNOW HE'LL SLEEP WELL, TOO...

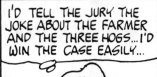

Z

ALL RIGHT, WHO MOVED THE TV?!

History of France

This is a report on Cardinal Rishhalleouooos.

"RISHHALLEOUOOOO"?

IF YOU DON'T KNOW HOW TO SPELL IT, FAKE IT!